Save Your Breath

Negotiate Better Deals by Talking Less

JANICE SETO

DEDICATION

Robin McQueen

My gratitude cannot be expressed
in words,
only
in chapters

CONTENTS

ACKNOWLEDGMENTS

My teachers

Mr Alistair Thompson (and Joan Thompson)

The late Mr Michael Kelly

Mr Bruce Ball

INTRODUCTION: Save Your breath

After a conference a few weeks ago, someone asked me how to go about being entrepreneurial. (Don't you love it when open-ended questions come your way just when there is a plane to be caught?) I gave a two-part yin-yang social-talk answer: "On the one hand, you have to cultivate being curious about the world around us and on the other hand, you have to filter in only what works for you." An open-and-shut response, a koan for him to think about.

In business, we are looking at opportunities all the time (I guess that is the politically-correct way to say we are always on the look out for deals). Entrepreneurs creatively put things together: the product or service with the end-user customer - and make payment fast and easy. That is basically all a deal is.

Just when I thought this was wrapped up, ready for filing, I got a followup. Giving it a minute of my attention to see what it was all about, I saw Millennial-speak: "Look, I don't know about your advice. I mean, I get what you said about opening my eyes and looking for what client needs are not being addressed. But I can't get on board with the deal making part. Like, I really don't like negotiating…"

I shot back, "That's because you are tired. I have watched you talk every minute of the day negotiating every darn thing. When you decide to filter out the trivial matters you currently negotiate, you save your breath for deals that are more worth your time and energy."

Then it struck me how much we can deplete ourselves when we indiscriminately think of every conversation as an opportunity to negotiate. Think of your breath and psychological energy as your life force that is as limited as today's hours of daylight. From this perspective, then make an intention to focus on the best use of your energy, to make the best deals. My good friend Mike Kellawan personifies this deliberate choice. He is self-aware at where he puts his energy and cordially lets others know too: "I'm not getting into a debate with you on this."

Let me share with you 9 ways you can save your breath, stop wasting your time, and negotiate better deals.

First, a quick note to talkers: some talkers are the worst negotiators because they negotiate everything. (Like this fellow who spoke to me.) These men and women talk too much. And often talk past the close. Then they don't any breath left to negotiate real deals.

Research by Deborah Tannen on speaking styles of men and women seem to indicate that women get much out of discussion as they derive emotional and cognitive benefits of 'talking it out'. The 'Tend and befriend' strategy most associated with women is the opposite of men who deal with stress by 'fight or flight'. It is not that all men are more succinct, some just do not derive much out of talking (*You're the Only One I Can Tell*).

The women and men who do enjoy talking and sparring can be more judicious with their time and energy and decide to talk when it counts.

Life's better when we leave the *Thinking Out Loud* to Ed Sheeran.

I can tell you this after years spent in hospitality. I also served two and a half years working in a job where I had to negotiate most hours, mostly high-stakes issues on behalf of clients. Sure, I was on one side of the table and the outcome did not affect me personally. One can remain indifferent and keep cool, if one chooses.

On the other hand, when I was in sales, I certainly had skin in the game. That's my compensation on the line!

In the education sector, it almost goes without saying that everyone wants to negotiate. Ditto in the hospitality industry. Born and raised in the family restaurant business, I often it useful to use the occasional food metaphor for deal-seeking, temper tantrum-tossing children (and adults).

As an entrepreneur, I have learnt to identify potential good deals, bad deals, deal makers and deal breakers.

These life lessons, well, there is a cost. Everyone learns through mistakes - those of others and those made by you.

May the following 9 tips (plus one bonus) shift the ratio above in your favour.

Chapter 1. Are the dealmakers in the room? Negotiate only with those who can negotiate.

Newsflash: It's not all negotiable.

For example: Never Negotiate with Children… You can reason with them, you could give them a short age-appropriate explanation, you may frame the big picture but adults never negotiate with children. Why? Because you can only negotiate with equals. Children are not equal to adults. Adults can get a marriage licence, a driver's licence, vote, get a job… and children cannot do the forementioned legally.

Now, as an adult parent, you have to think things through. Think into the future. As Dr Phil McGraw has said, "You are not raising children, you are raising adults." What do adults do? They are accountable for their actions, learn skills to make a living, and are responsible for making a home that nurtures their children, directs their actions, and channels their energy and their growth potential.

So you have to make sure they know YOU are the grown up in the room – and they have to be told there are things they cannot possibly know at their young age and your duty is to be that shield. You are just doing your job.

The facts of life is that this world is based on reality, not on entitlements.

Are the people who want to negotiate the ones who can sign off on it? If they are not, and you know it, and are only doing this to be kind, then it is a total waste of your time. Lygia Dallip, previously with the Ministry of Education, Ontario, shared this insight with me years ago and it has spared me expending valuable time on things that won't pay off.

To bring this point home: Too many parents waste time negotiating with their offspring. Unless they pay rent and the utility bills, buy the groceries, have a licence to drive, and are no living under your roof... bottom line, they are not in a position to negotiate.

Don't compensate by giving them that platform.

Don't give them the power they should not have.

There is a power imbalance because you are the adult with adult responsibilities. Your job as a parent is to raise adults who have a chance of making it in the real world. So you have to make sure they know YOU are the grown up in the room – and they have to be told there are things they cannot possibly know at their young age and your duty is to be that shield.

You are just doing your job. That includes putting a limit their cell phone use, refuse Game of Thrones, and demand respectful behaviour. Their job as children is to work themselves out of your home through education and entrepreneurship and/or job.

When I was babysitting my toddler niece and nephew one day, they came up to me saying "We do not want to make our bed."

My response: "In life, there are things you want to do and things you Have to do... You have to make your bed." End of discussion.

The facts of life is that this world is based on reality, not on entitlements. Feel free to explain that to children and give them one opportunity to be listened to… but in the end, it's your call as you are the mature adult in the room.

What if your children are Boomerang offspring? The same applies, regardless of age. Your roof, your rules.

Chapter 2. Is this YOUR issue? (or someone else's who want the extrovert to do the dirty work)

I spent two and a half years in that job negotiating the issues of clients every day. The reason I did it was the firm had me on salary. Would I have brought my A-game to work with a room of often semi-deranged people if I had not been <u>paid</u> for my pains? No way.

Sometimes your generous heart prompts you to give freebies of your time. I have been there and I still do it. On occasion. As long as there is a tangential tie to me, it is worth my time. But if it is someone else's and there is the potential it could devolve into 'shoot the messenger', let the stakeholders take care of their own.

Decide if it is even your issue (walk away). Here are two examples, one done well, and the other, well, I took the sucker's choice.

In the first, it was my first independent apartment after graduating. I was having a problem with my apartment mate (and perhaps she had issues with me, though hard to see why). Anyways, I asked our landlord to be a witness or mediator or some other undefined role to ensure we kept on topic. He phoned a few minutes before our meeting – and said he would not be there as it was not his place.

Now, I think he should have given more notice… but I give him the benefit of the doubt that this was the best he could do.

In the second, the head of the department emailed to break some sad news to one of my classes and negotiate rescheduling. I was tasked with telling them that the previous instructor of this course was now the late instructor of the course and schedules had to be amended.

As no senior staff would do it, the department head decided to give this dirty work to the new hire. At that time, I had a reputation of someone who liked to talk (I was such an amateur). I thought I was stepping up to the plate in taking it on.

Ha!

I was hopping onto the firing line. No surprise that I left that job a few months later. Any management team that sets up the new hire to take the fall isn't worth sticking around for. No surprise that the other people hired similar to me – we need fresh blood to bring about much-needed change - all got jobs elsewhere.

Chapter 3. Is this worth negotiating? What's NOT Negotiable

Occasionally an opportunity adds to being a deal that is either too small for the expenditure of effort or it is a one-off that won't lead anywhere else.

Some people like to throw all their time and energy into negotiating every tiny, minute thing just to prove a point. They get carried away by the emotional high of winning that it gets so out of proportion to the value of the deal.

Fellas, you just want to make your point - or as I call it, your Pyrrhic victory. I prefer to negotiate to make profit.

Chapter 4. Is there someone else better to Negotiate?

You want to get involved in negotiations when you are not the ideal person around the table.

The best person may have the extra leverage of a law degree. There may be a tax accountant whose expertise in the tax code is of utmost important – you know that even if the other side does not. And sometimes it is as mysterious as they speak the same language (professional or linguistic).

It is a sign of maturity to cede the floor gracefully to another dealmaker.

Chapter 5. Have you read the experts?

Natural negotiators got there by… practice and reading up on the experts. Most in the field recommend *Getting to Yes*, the classic on interest-based negotiations. It is logical and methodical and win-win. Some lean towards Chris Voss's *Never Split the Difference* whose prowess comes from his time as the FBI's lead hostage negotiator. It recognizes emotions in the negotiation process and expands your skillset with practical tips.

Also highly recommended are *Crucial Conversations* and its companion book *Crucial Accountability* by the VitalWorks team. From personal experience, their training workshops are well worth your time and investment in yourself.

If you can get a hold of the book and the workbook for *Boundaries* by Drs Henry Cloud and John Townsend, you do yourself a big favour.

To really raise eyebrows on the commuter train, take out Robert Sutton's *No Asshole Rule* and *The Asshole Survival Guide* - they will also raise your game.

Chapter 6. Is the other side serious about doing a deal?

"Life's too short for x" Are you negotiating with the right person - Who holds the cards? Identifying the key decision maker is important

Some people just want to hear themselves talk. Or let you know "I am really important." Or have time to waste and get off wanting to see what work looks like – and you are giving them a demonstration. (In sales, we often don't know who is serious about doing a deal so sometimes you want to err on the side of caution and take EVERYONE seriously. But giving indiscriminate benefit of the doubt saps your energy. That's why we in sales qualify the lead very early in the interaction. We qualify if this person is in the position to buy (Decision maker) and how likely this person is to buy today. It saves you time and let's them go on their way to waste the time of a novice salesperson.

Identify quickly if the other side wants to fight or to sign. In short: Is their agenda to fight against a deal rather than negotiate a deal?

If they are not the persons who can close the deal or if the other side just wants to get some entertainment out of your sincere efforts (rather foul of them…), then they aren't serious about reaching a deal. They just like the process of hearing themselves get off a few bon mots in front of an audience. Yes, they really insecure that way. Talking and pitching to these people is a total waste of your time.

Another flavor is: Are you negotiating with the Problem Child or the Favourite Child? Efforts and results are not equally valued… and carrying out the terms of the deal could be a slog or smooth sailing depending on their status with the other side. If deals negotiated by the Problem Child are not taken seriously by the other side, then it is a waste of your time.

Chapter 7. What's the word on the street about the other side?

If the other side has the reputation as an emotional vampire or could audition for a lead in Robert Sutton's bestsellers, you best heed the warning of the low level of trustworthiness of the other side.

If the person is insane or just acts insane, don't negotiate with them. The best strategy is to save yourself and put distance between you. Whether that means walking away from the negotiating table, dissolving the partnership, getting another vender, consulting a divorce lawyer, updating your resume/CV, or getting entrepreneurial, dealing with someone nuts wastes your time, save your breath and bail.

In *The Caine Mutiny*, the crew found out that using logic with someone nuts does not work – and everyone on board gets caught in the undertow. You can ignore them and whatever enticements like job, benefits, opportunities, and make them disappear from your life.

Low maintenance people are better to deal with and make deals with. They are out there. "I got slimed" is funny on Ghostbusters, but in real life, a deal everyone agrees to and sticks to is a great metaphor!

Chapter 8. What's the word on the street about your side? Whom do they think they are dealing with?

This follows on the previous tip: your reputation as a trustworthy negotiator will attract people who want to deal with you. Trustworthy does not mean someone who caves in easily but someone of judgement and maturity who is organized.

You respect all the preparation and research that goes into making deals and enter negotiations respecting their time and effort too. If you have a reputation as a creative and cordial negotiator, all the better.

We get people seeking us out all the time because their time is valuable. Dealing with likeminded people - Monty Hall's line was Let's Make a Deal! - quickens the pace of negotiations because no one in the room has time to waste. We get to the point.

Chapter 9. What else is there beside the dollar figure?

If everything in the deal is all about money, then you either have it or you don't.

It is worth a few back-and-forths, however, if all sides are up for exploring any non-money items. Those who are open to outside-the-box creative deals that increase the satisfaction of all stakeholders get more than a deal. They gain a reputation.

A few common-sense tips on setting the stage for creative win-win deals amidst a respectful atmosphere:

- Place – A neutral location or preferably your own turf. Even the golf course, dinner, cruise
- Time - clear your schedule. Pretend you are at the dentist's and have no idea how long it will take. You do not want to curtail momentum. At the same time, you don't want the other side to know you are open-ended
- Who is there -> witnesses (3 times refusal)
- Have a draft ready (and three pens)
- Money and other items that are not $ (conditions)
- Trust - or are you giving just the first taste of a problem person...?
- Consider leaving something on the table that contributes to win-win

You can't have everything, don't hold out for the impossible. The preferred approach to the deal is to get the maximum win-win possible. Why live the regret of not extending your reach?

Chapter 10. Deal Me Out of this Deal

Sometimes the best deal you can get is to get out of the country in one piece.

When a good deal goes sour when it comes to performance and accountability or internal politics, you have just gotten a window on the character of the other side. This becomes a clean up case, or a case for a clean break. Getting out of a partnership that has gone bad is the goal: no amount of cinnamon topping is going to make this coffee taste good.

Two words: Get Out

Three words: Get Out Now

Four words: And Don't Go Back

As a negotiator, you may have to leave money on the table in order to get your client or yourself out of this horrible situation. When divorce is the only option, you may have to buy your way back to sanity (professionally or martially). But at least you get closure and the deal-gone-bad is over.

Some people would advise their clients to stay in chronic psychological pain for the sake of their own ego. I just don't buy into prolonging a hopeless situation that we had tried to change. Some organizations just do not evolve, as much as they say so. Do not take them at their word, look at their actions. Then take action.

As Kenny Rogers sang in The Gambler: Know when to hold em, know when to fold em.

Save your breath. Say your good-byes. Tomorrow is another day to seek out better deals.

Bonus: Useful Phrases and Tips for Negotiations

1. "I know it, you know it…"
2. "Let's You and Me hammer it out while others wait outside…"
3. Me to Client -> "Let me do the talking"
4. "He's only MY client because You hired him…"
5. "Patience, young Jedi" ie Let the process unfold… or it will cost you.
6. Mike drop -> "I wasn't going to get a reference from these a$$h@les so execute your exit strategy…"
7. "I'm afraid we can't help you…"
8. " I wish I could do that but I Can't…"
9. Confidentiality phrase "It's all settled and that's all I can say" (Flash a smile)

10. Don't take insults (or flattery) personally -> Janice's dad owned a restaurant...

11. Never negotiate with children : "In life, there are things you want to do and things you Have to do... You have to make your bed." End of discussion.

12. "Keep your trap shut when the boss is talking... that way you can learn…"

13. "Don't go for broke -> learn the other side's limit."

14. "Don't hang around complainers and amateurs."

15. "Give everyone one chance and then haul anchor cause the fish ain't biting."

16. "Know who REALLY calls the shots…"

17. "Get out when the gettin's good -> someone else offers you a good deal on something u want to unload…"

18. "You can walk away... if you keep your eye on the long term puck… " Keep turning down deals that are meh

19. "Be prepared to play hardball if they won't play ball..."

20. Words of wisdom from my late father, Johnny Seto, "We didn't go through all that crap of immigrating and adjusting to a new country so that you put up with crap at work. Get a better job..."

21. "Is there any movement on X issue..."

22. "Is there any appetite for...?"

23. "I tried to like that truffle sauce (substitute name of any awful dish at a restaurant)…"

24. "Can you check if they could come back with something a bit more...? You know I am a low-maintenance loyal customer who refers people to you..."

25. Don't ask for favours, give reasons

26. Remind your client that only YOU are on their side... when stakes are very high, they sometimes forget

27. Once a negotiation is done, it's done. You can't go back and seek to do it over.

28. If there is stark bias or egregious lies, let them know you can default to litigation: "You'll hear from my lawyer..."

29. If your side cannot get the paperwork straight, and keep giving me changes to initial, I am going to stop signing and start calling your staff's competence (and by the way, YOURS) into question.

Treasure a positive outlook:
the best deals are the rewards of saving your breath.

###

ABOUT THE AUTHOR

Janice Seto has hammered out deals in various capacities: real estate, business, human resources, and union-labour environments. Her reputation is of a selfless negotiator, looking out for the best interest of the client. Along the way, she has won some and lost some – and learnt enough strategies to pass on in this book to those who want to make the best use of their time and save their breath for serious deals.

Janice Seto writes non-fiction and commentary including articles for The Bridge, the publication of The Malaysia-Canada Business Council.

Her more recent books are also available on Amazon: *Standing Out in The Background – A Guide to Extra Work in Toronto's Film & TV Industry* and *Johnny Seto's Bowmanville – An Enneagram Perspective*. The System for Women is her first book series on relationships. *Walking for Clean Water: Pukatawagan on the Move* is a bilingual English-Cree illustrated children's book by Janice Seto, with the Cree translation by Ralph Caribou.

Bowmanville's Octagon House – From Church and Faith and Tait to Irwin & Seto went all the way to #1 on the Amazon Bestseller list free download in its category during Easter 2017.

www.ingramcontent.com/pod-product-compliance
Lightning Source LLC
Chambersburg PA
CBHW060514200326
41520CB00017B/5040